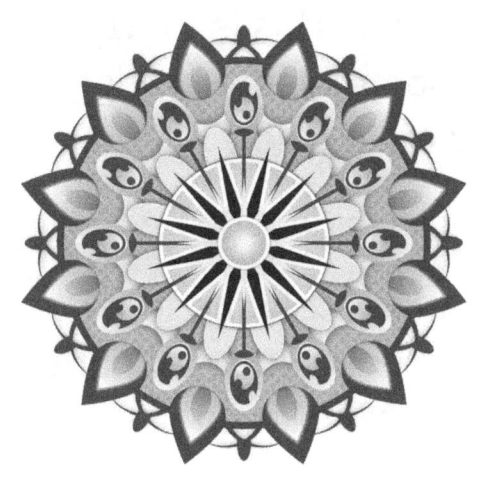

CREATIVELY COLORING

ISBN-13: 978-1532958786
ISBN-10: 1532958781

COLORING THIS BOOK

Before you get started here are a few points to take note of;

One-Sided Pages

The back of each picture is blank. This is to help prevent bleed-through destroying the next picture. Some bleed-through will occur but it should not affect the next picture you want to color.

Separating Sheet

If your particular markers or other coloring tool *does* bleed through excessively then please consider taking a loose sheet of paper and using this as extra padding behind the page you are coloring

Photocopying

Since this is your book you might want to consider photocopying the pictures and coloring that version. That way you still have an uncolored book in your posession.

The Patterns

The patterns in this book are all full-page. They have been selected to provide variety and a mix of challenges. There are organic flowing patterns and angular geometric patterns, simple repeating and complex overlapping. Some are simple shapes that repeat many tmes while others are comlex patterns that might only repeat a part of its design. All will provide you with enjoyment.

When you're finished with this book check out our other books, our Instagram account (@creativelycoloring) and the club (www.creativelycoloring.com) where you can get free downloads and video tutorials.

Show Us Your Finished Results

Creatively Coloring is one of the largest coloring accounts on Instagram. With tens of thousands of followers we are lucky to be able to showcase some of the best coloring around the world. We would love to see your finished work.

To let us know they are available post them on Instagram with the hashtag #creativelycoloring or @creativelycoloring

Join The FREE Creatively Coloring Club

- FREE TUTORIAL VIDEOS
- FREE COLORING BOOKS AND PAGES
- GREAT COMPETITIONS
- EXCLUSIVE DISCOUNTS

In addition to the Instagram account we also have a rapidly growing club at creativelycoloring.com. This is a free resource that includes tutorial videos and regular free books, pages and competitions.

Come and join us at www.creativelycoloring.com

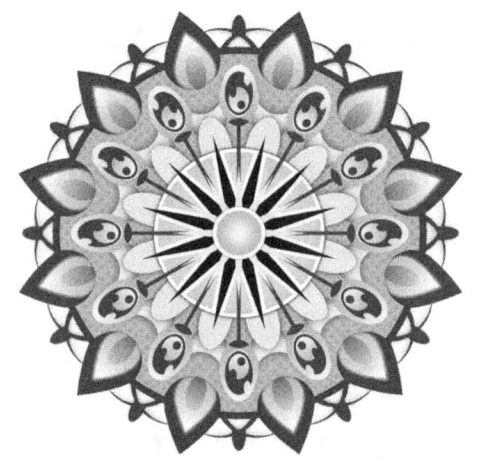

PATTERN PARTY #2

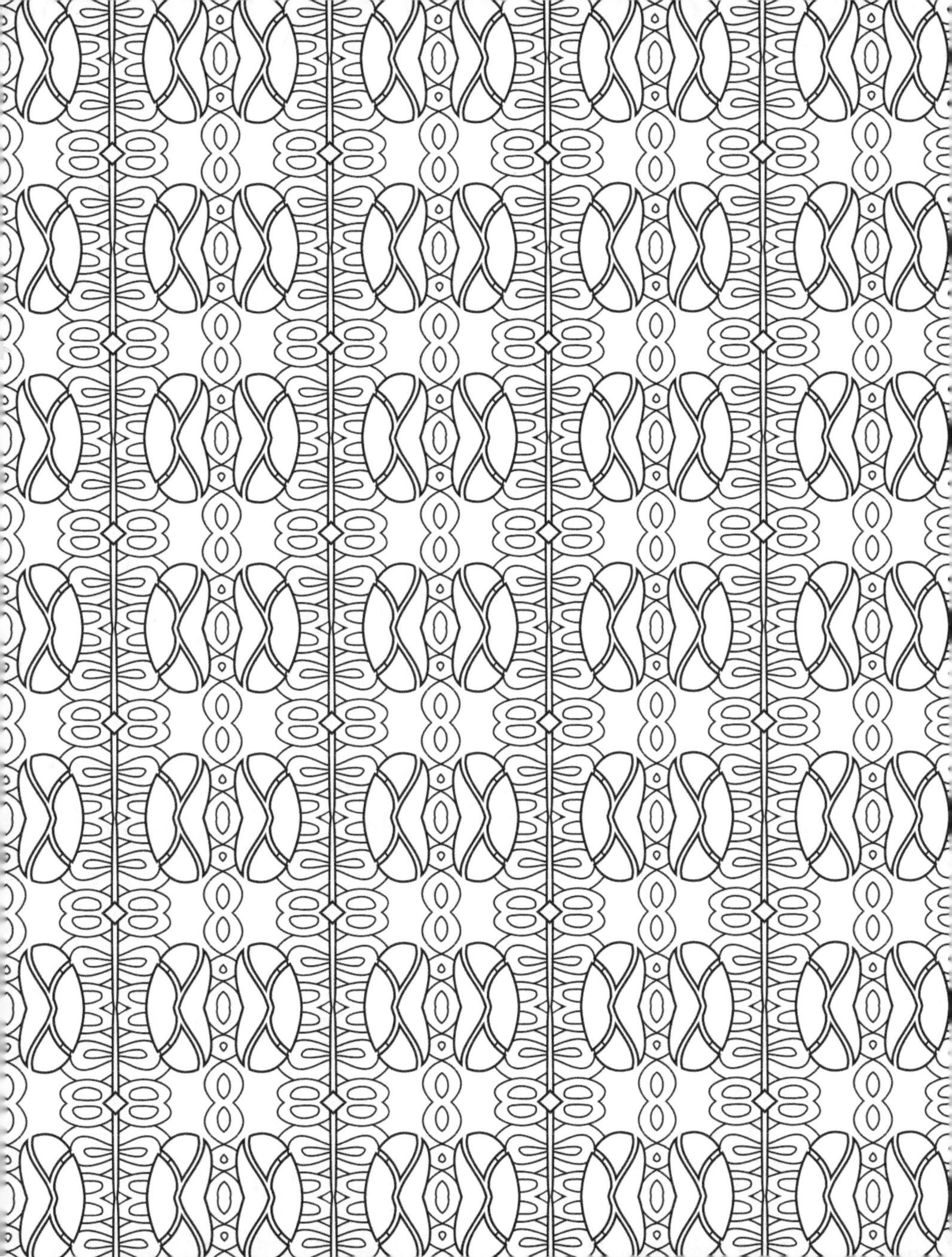

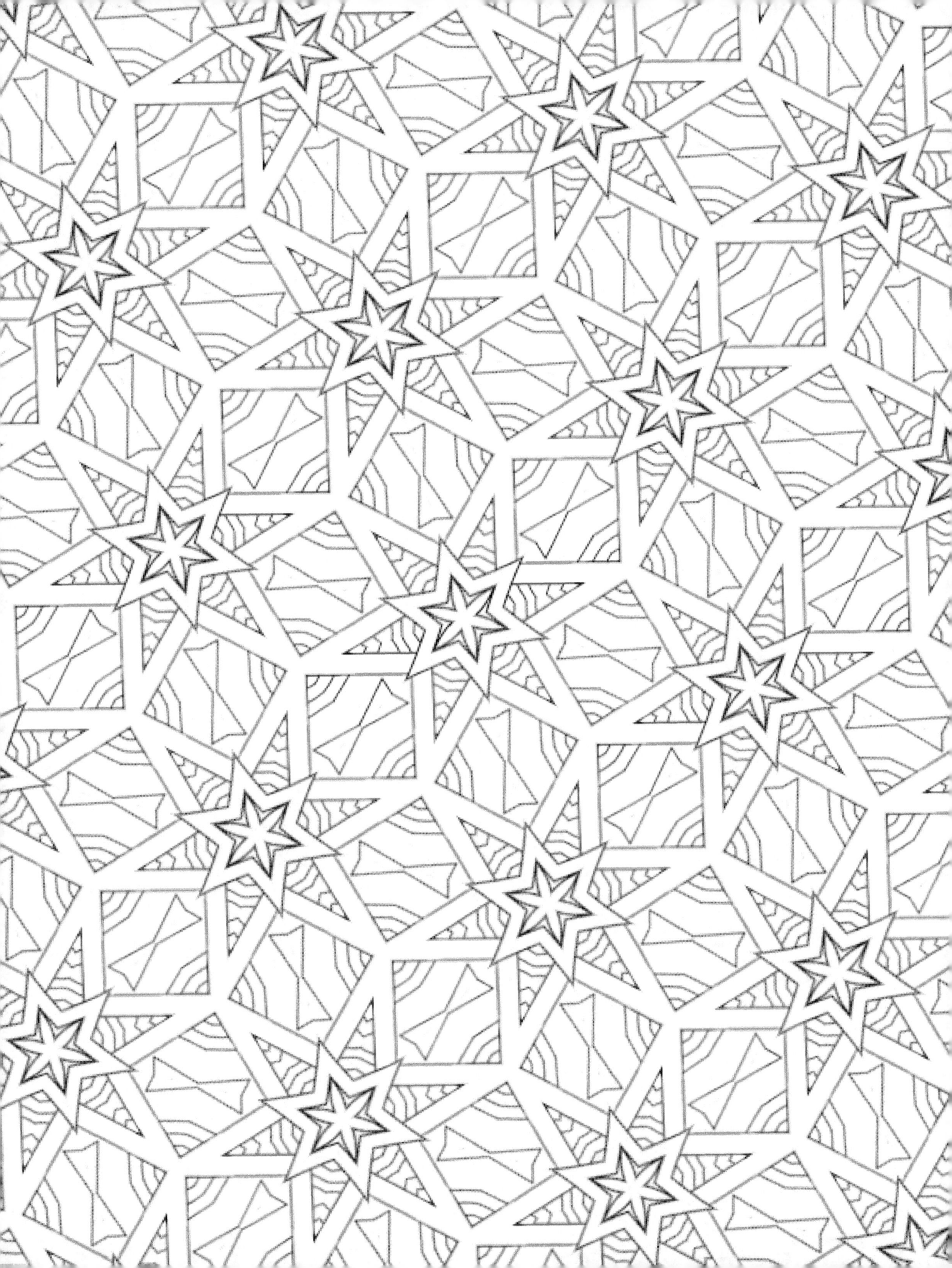

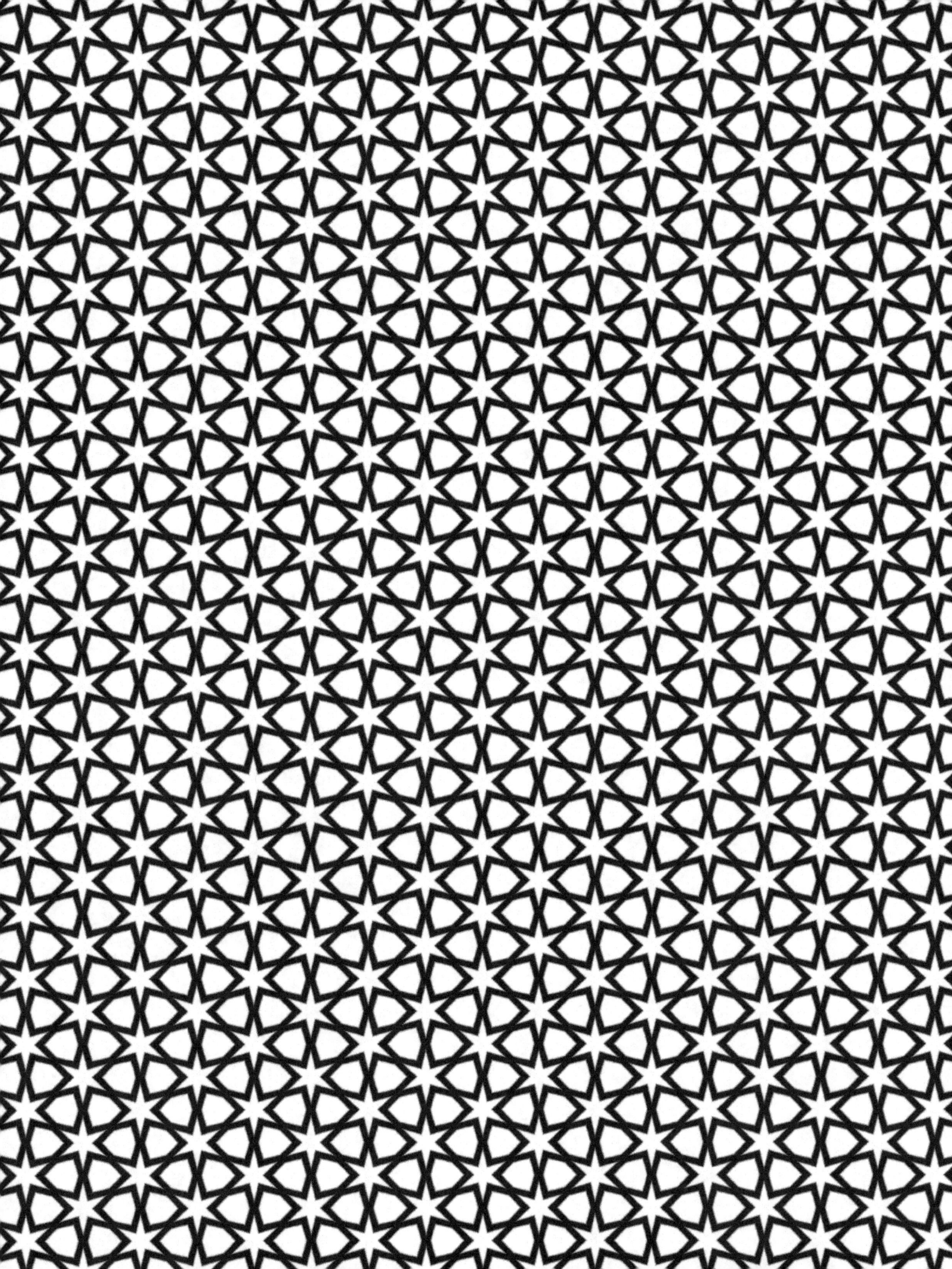

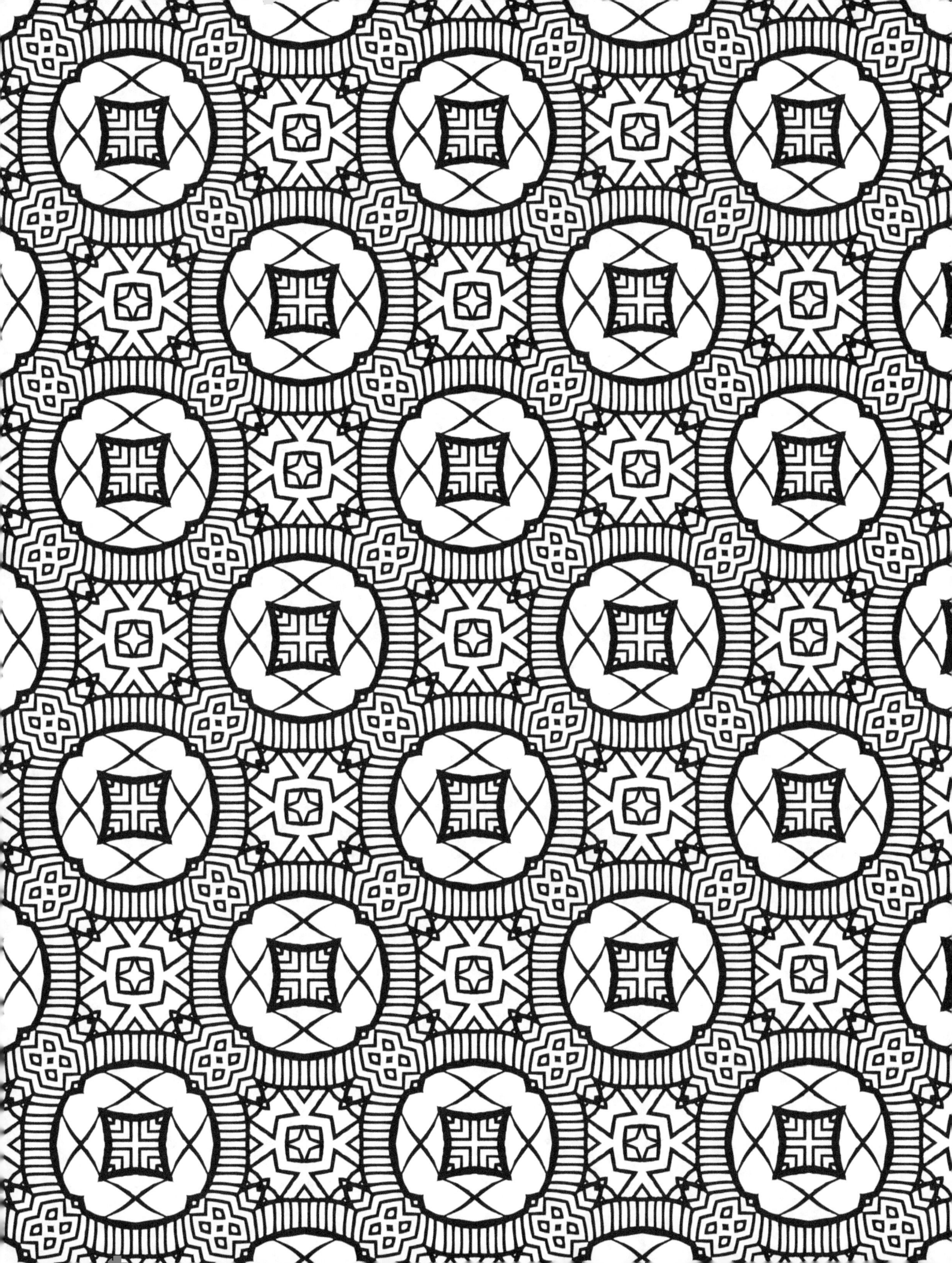

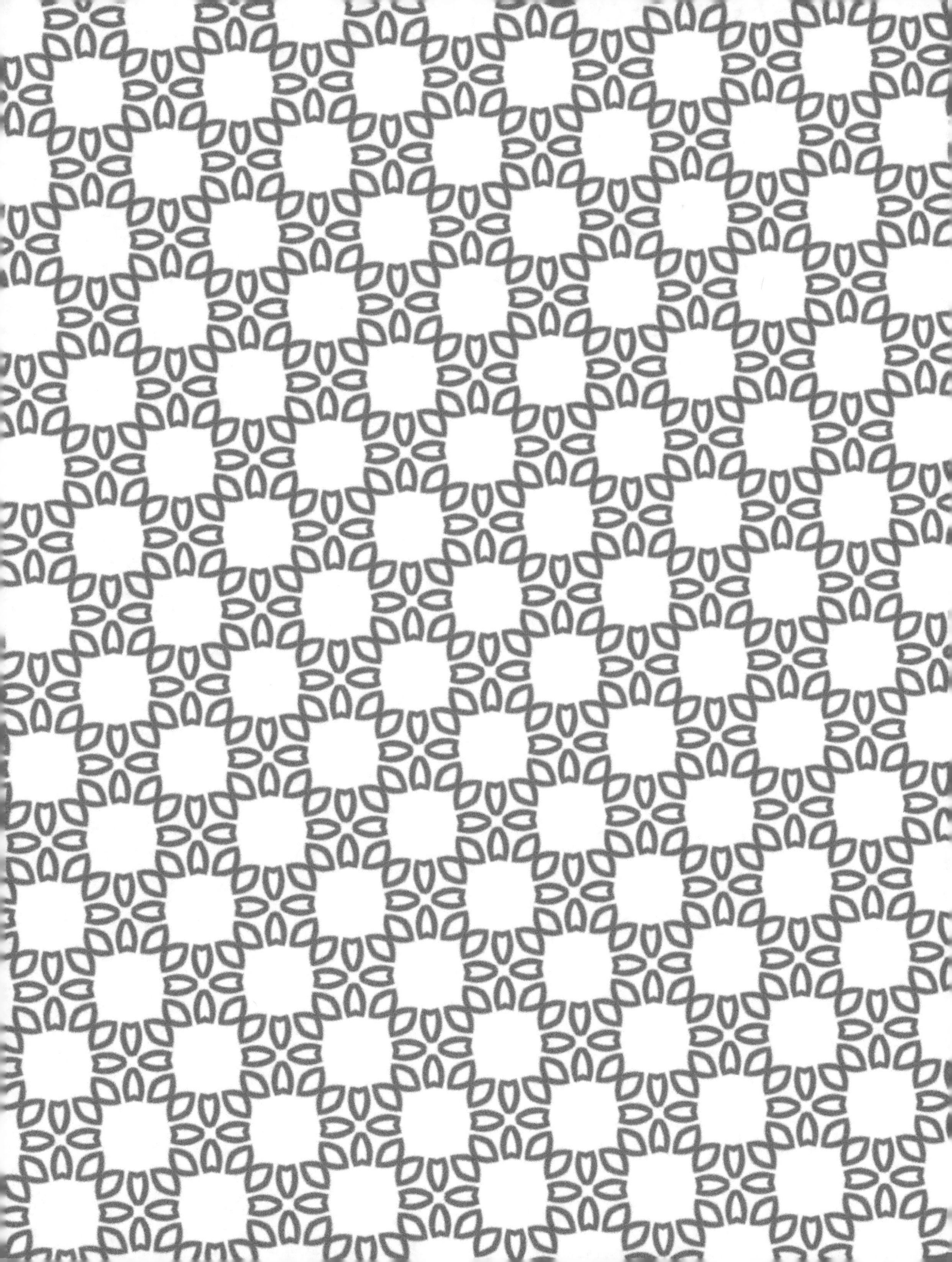

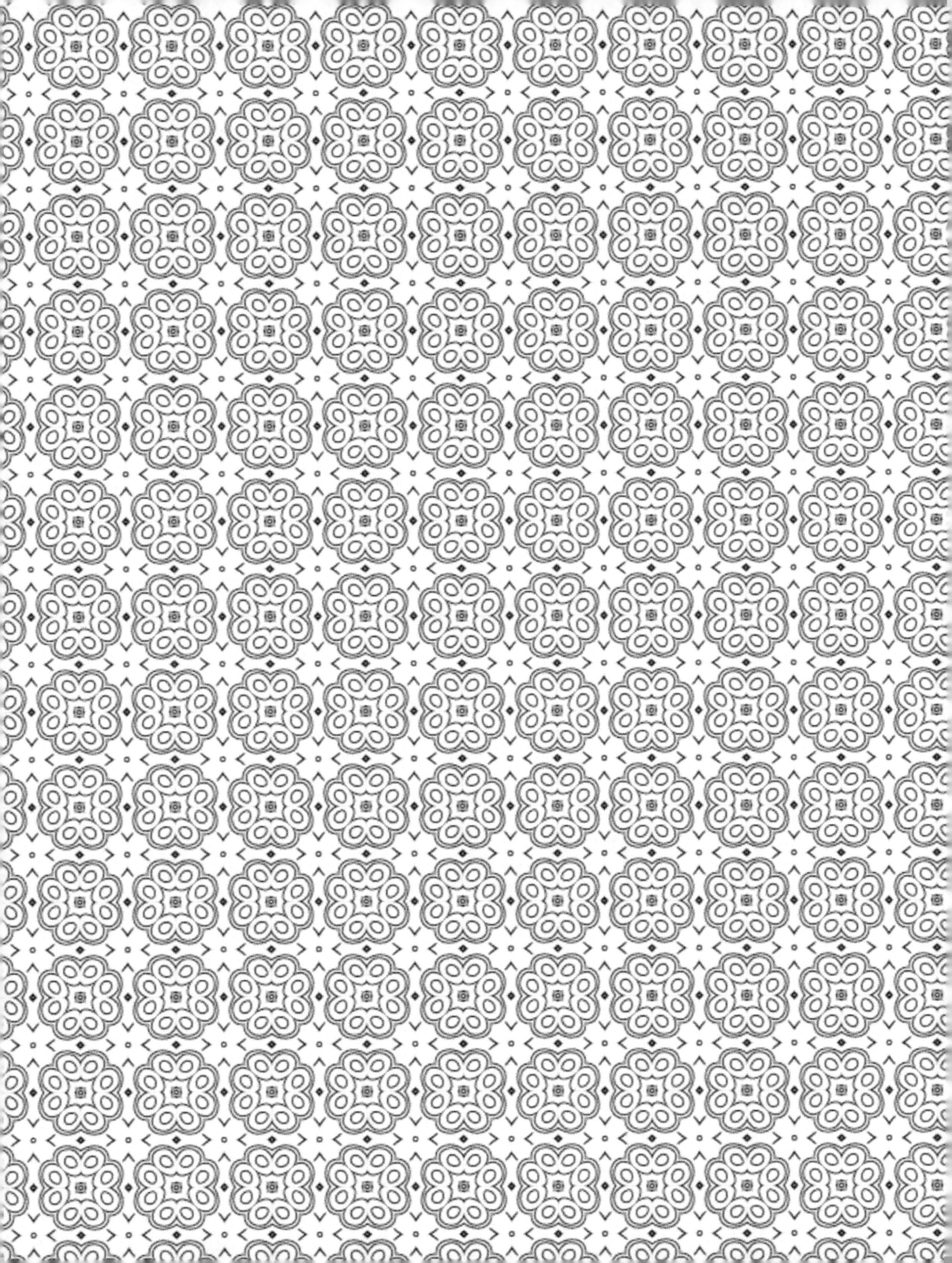

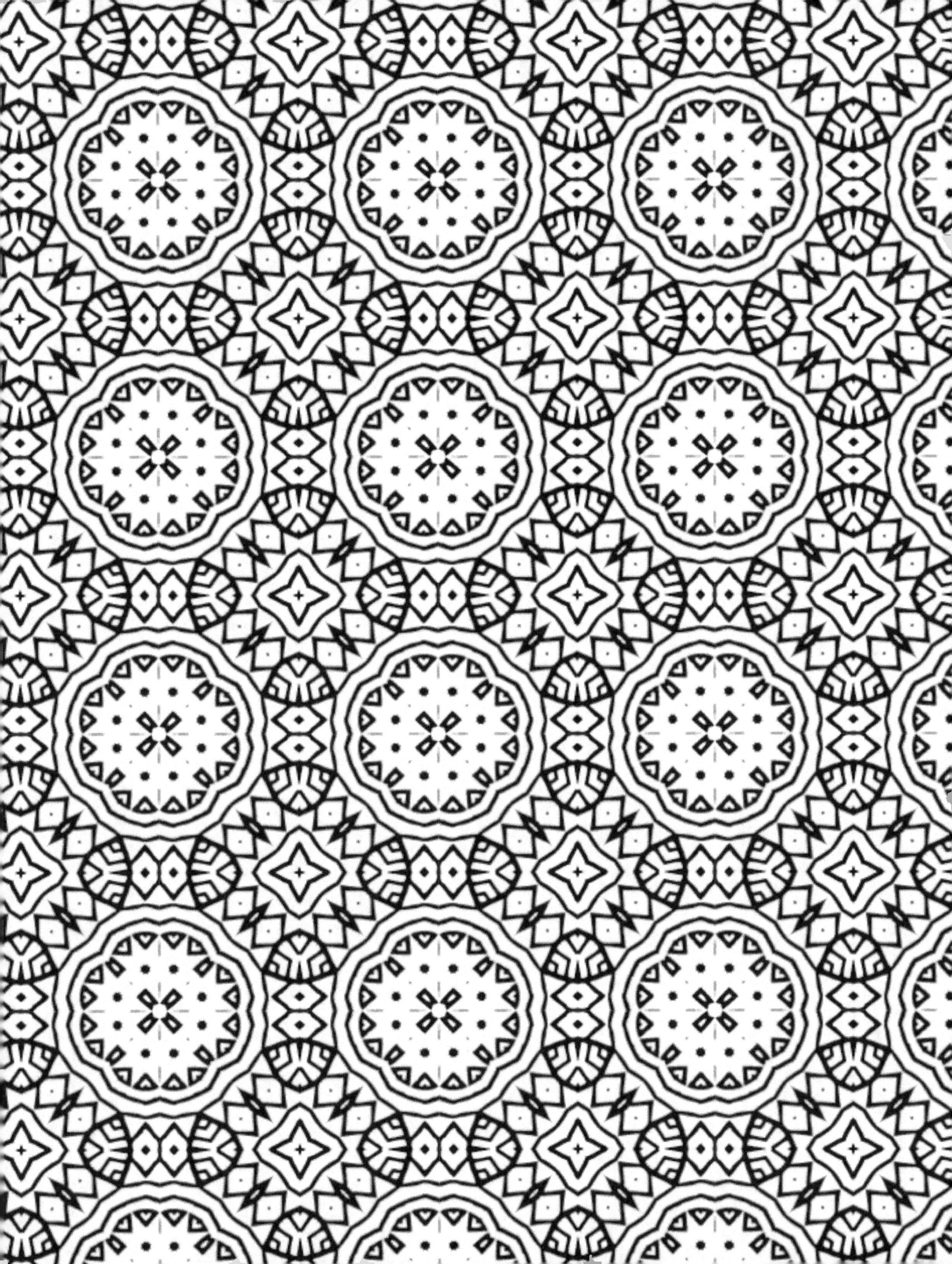

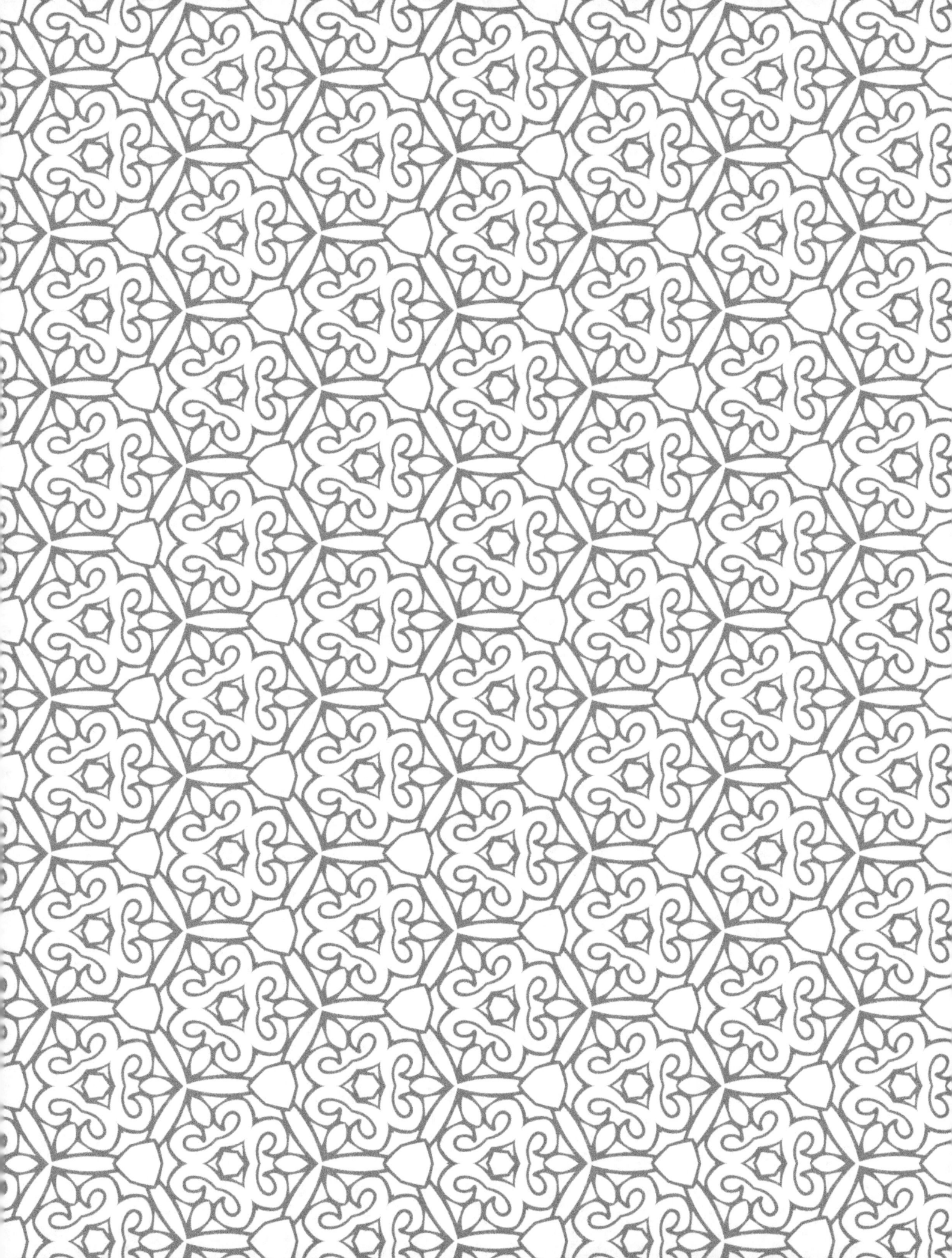

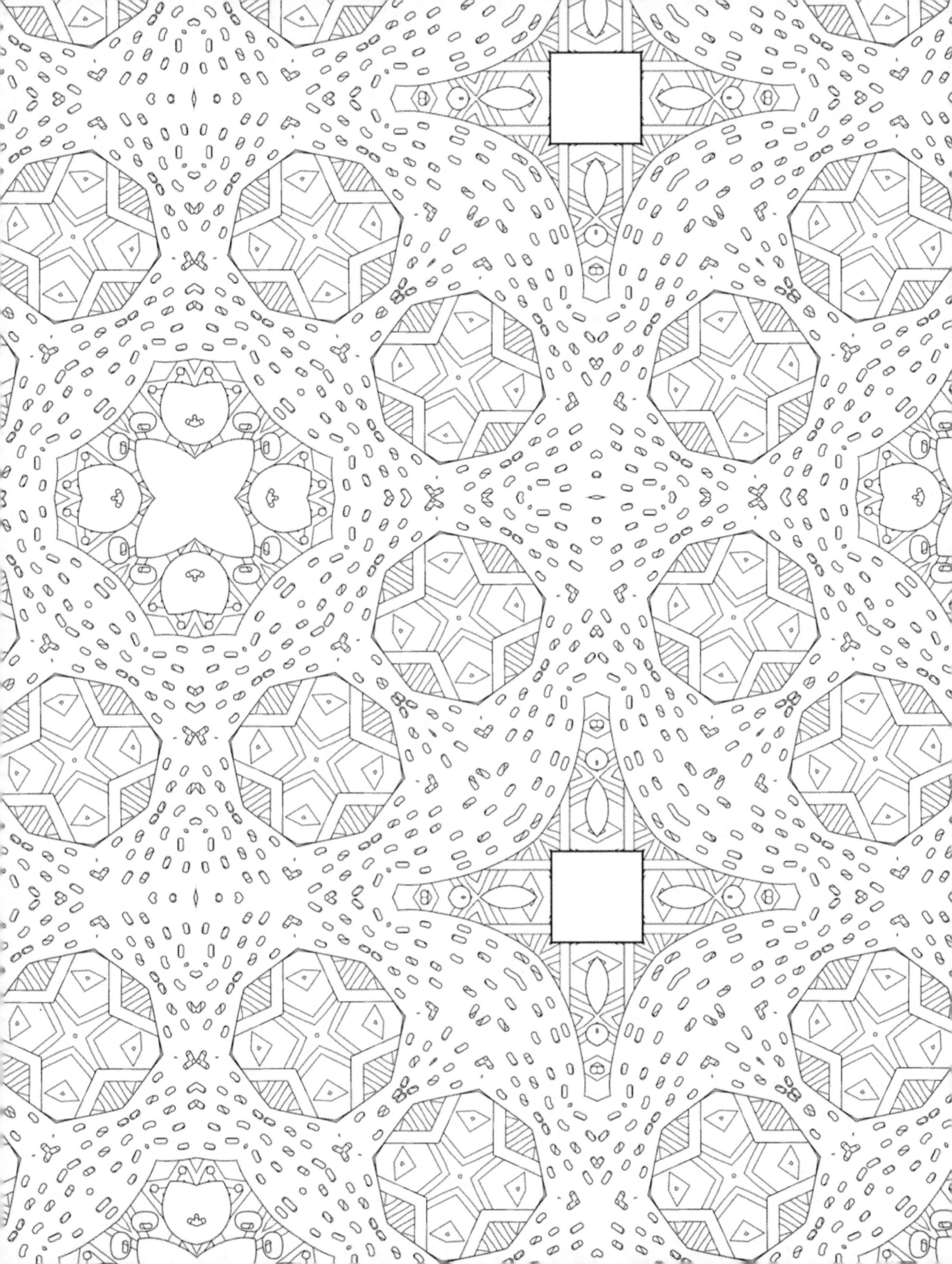

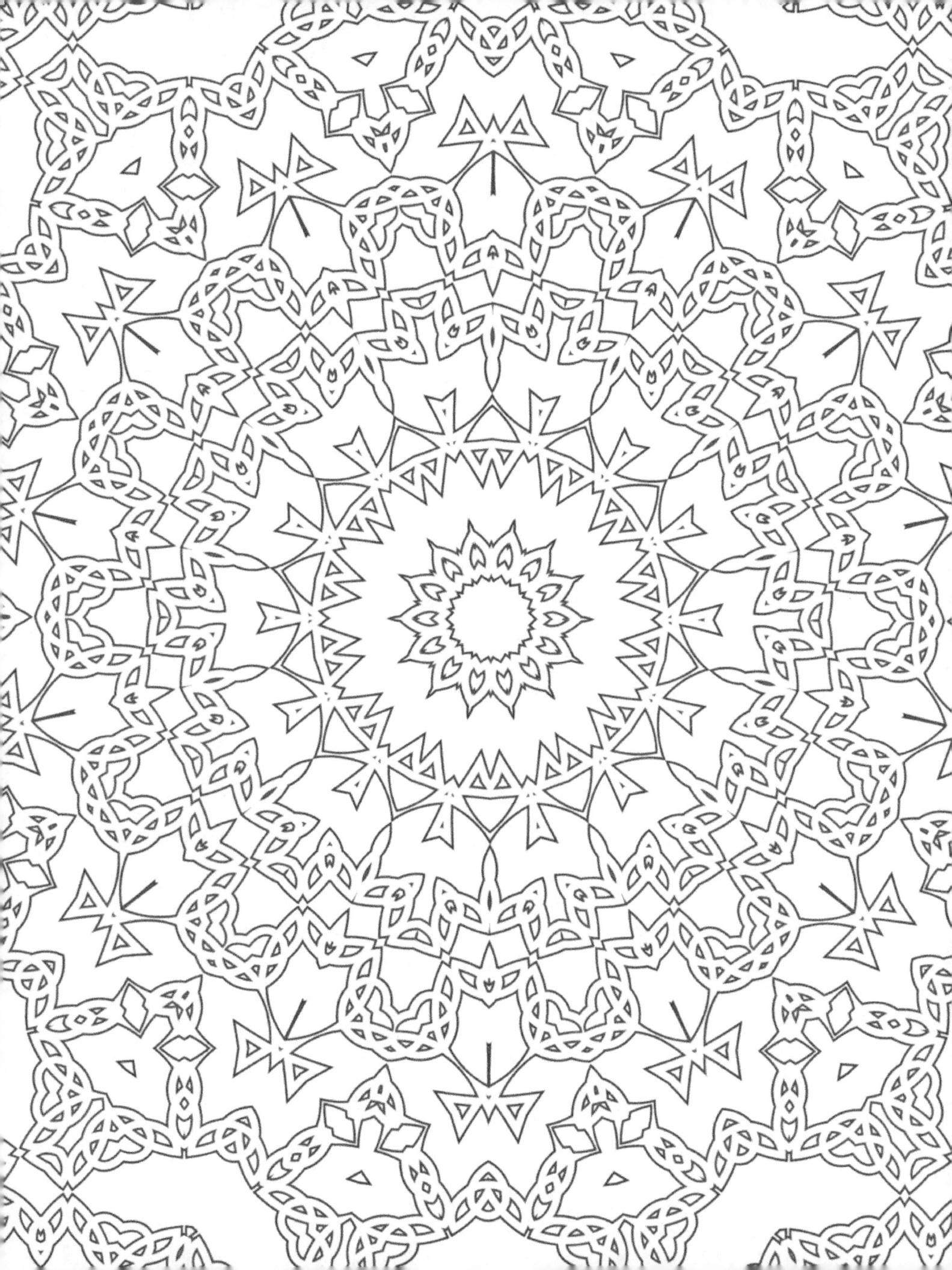

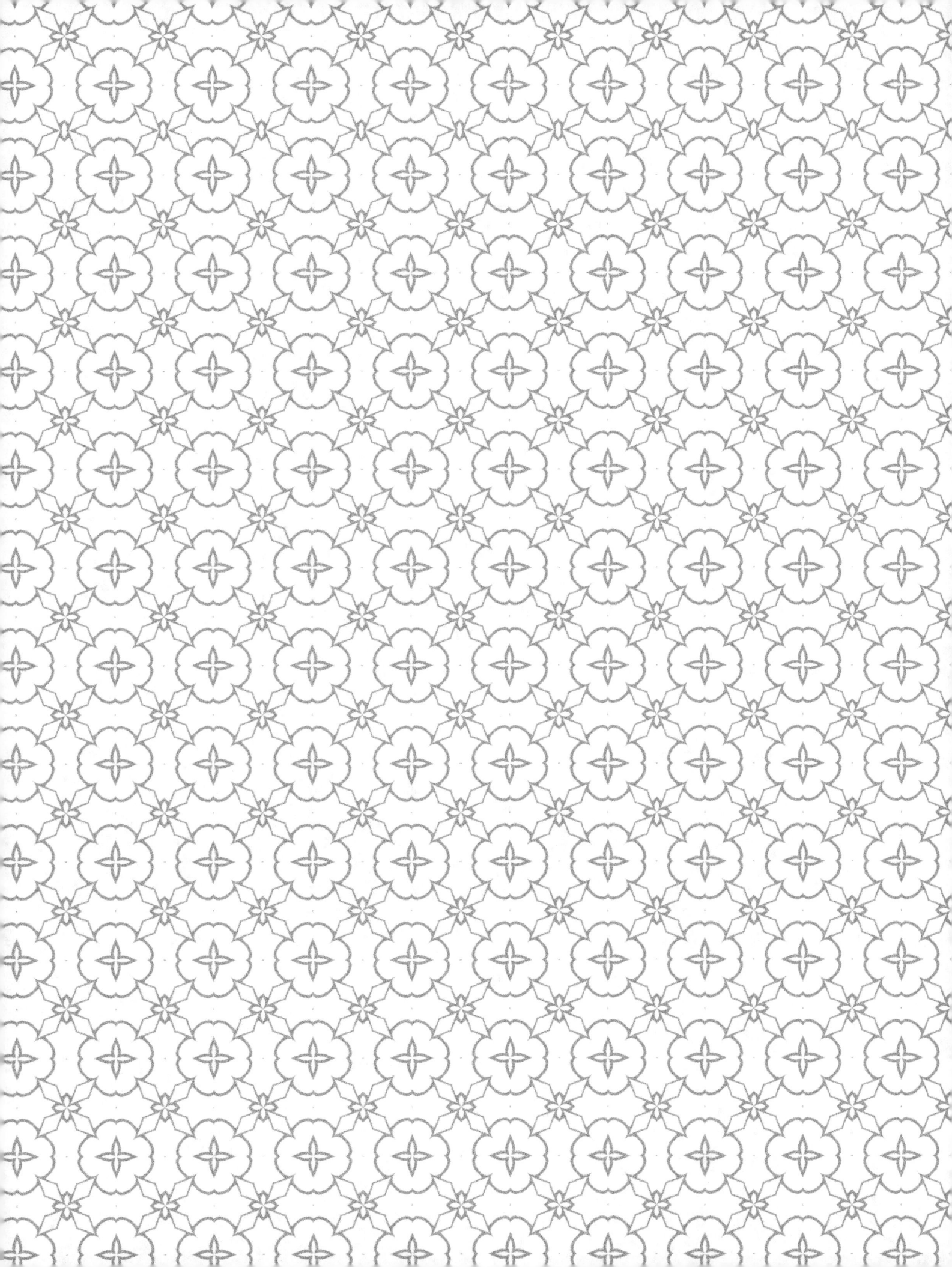

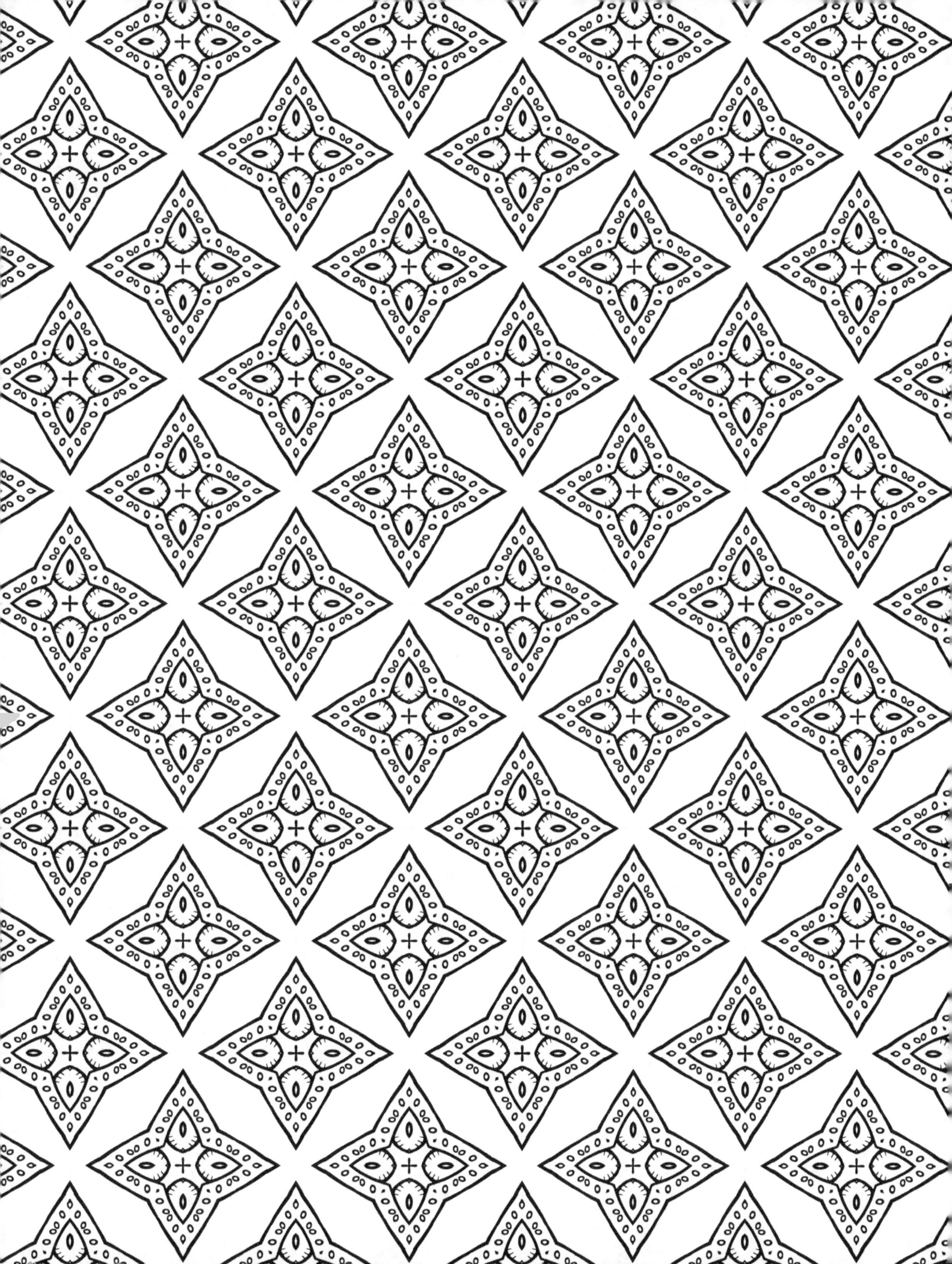

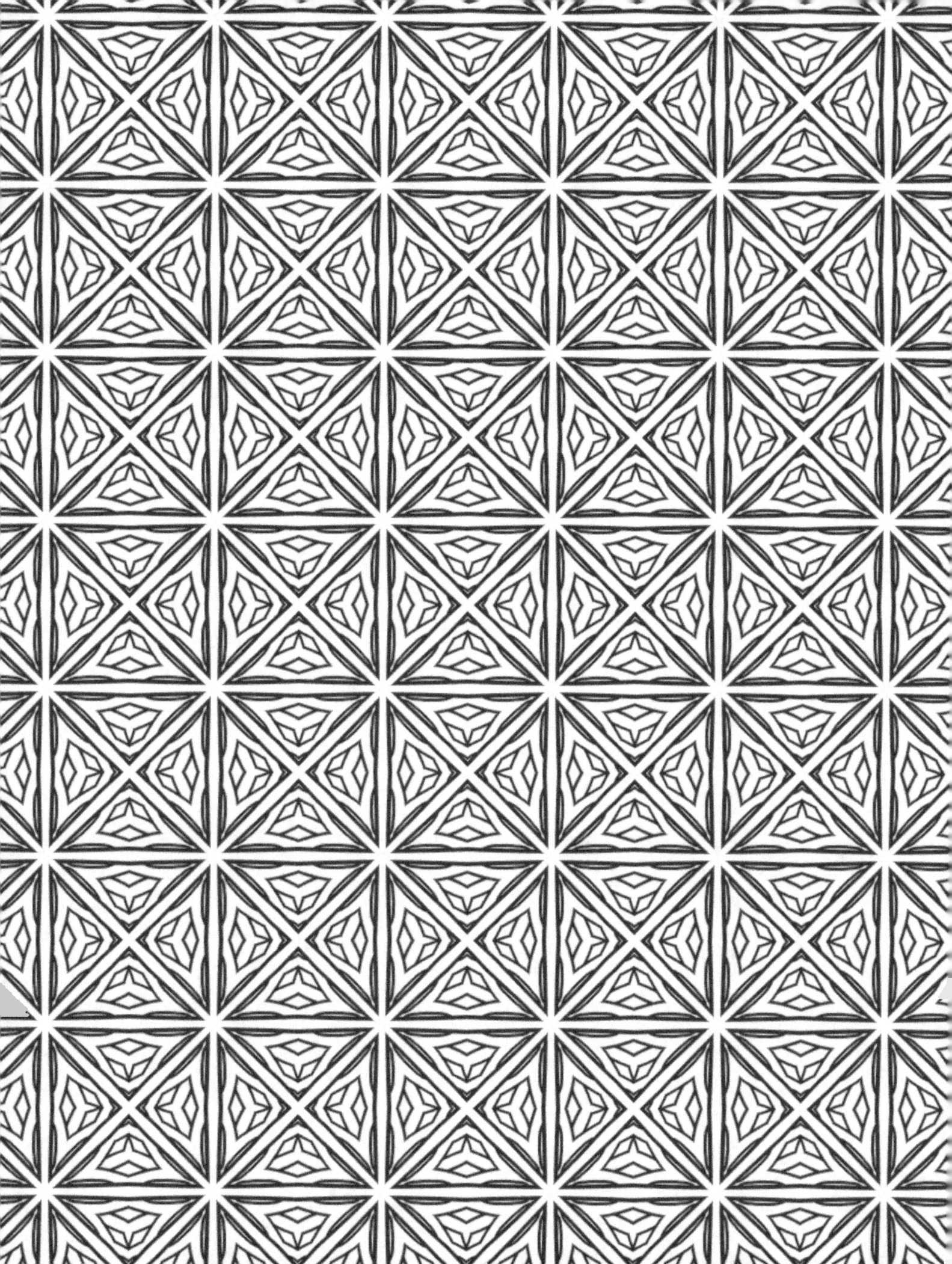

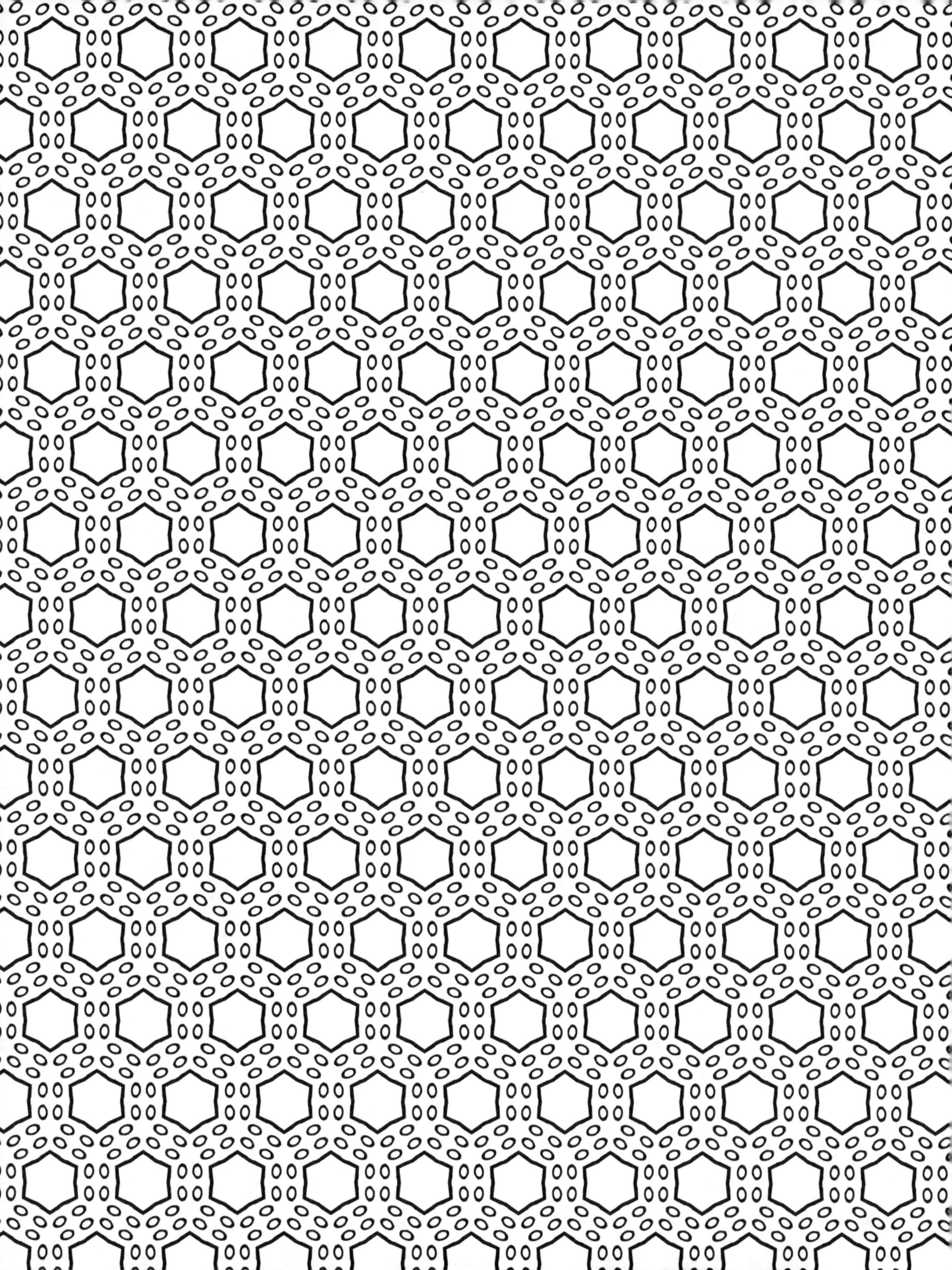

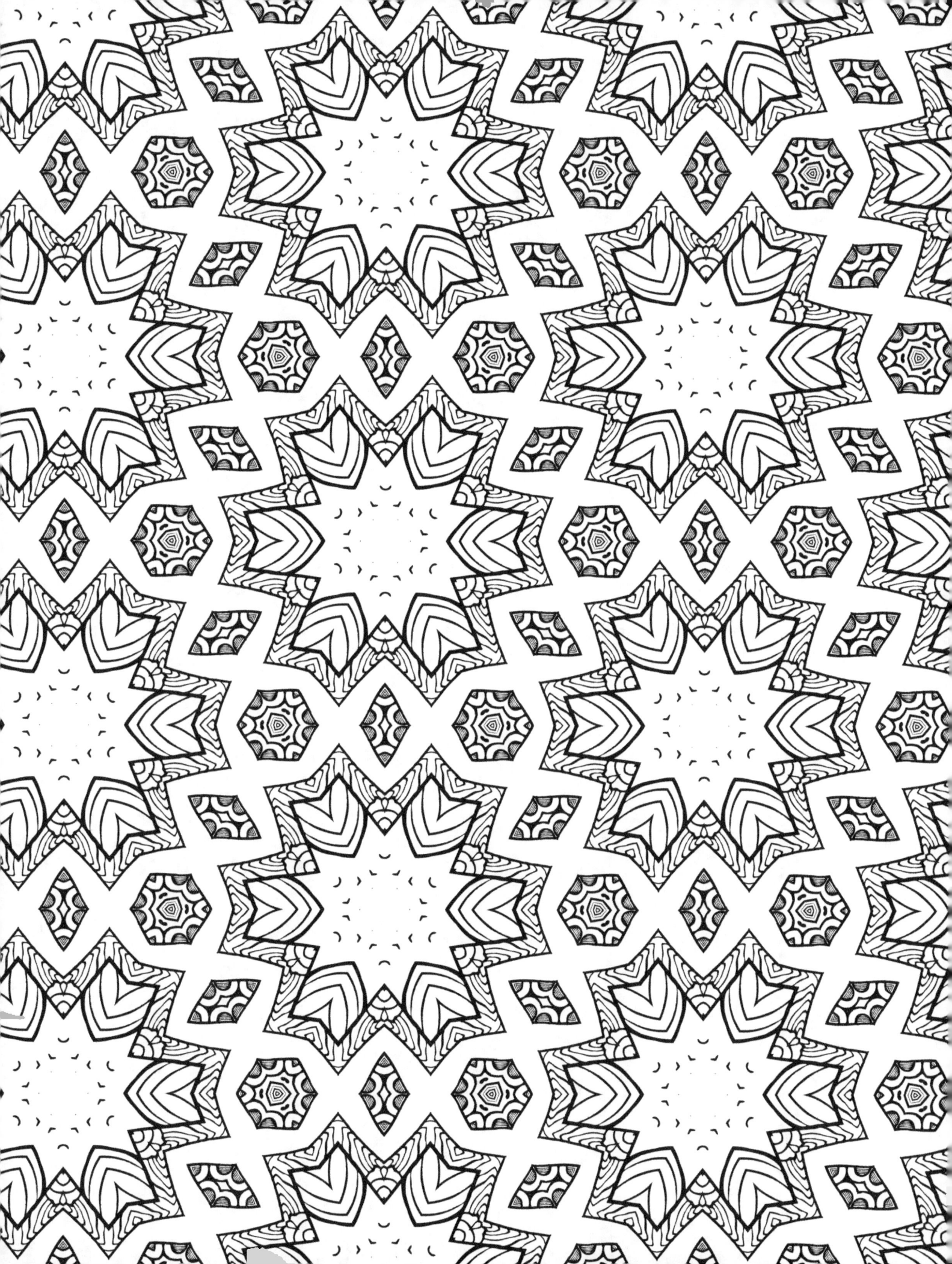

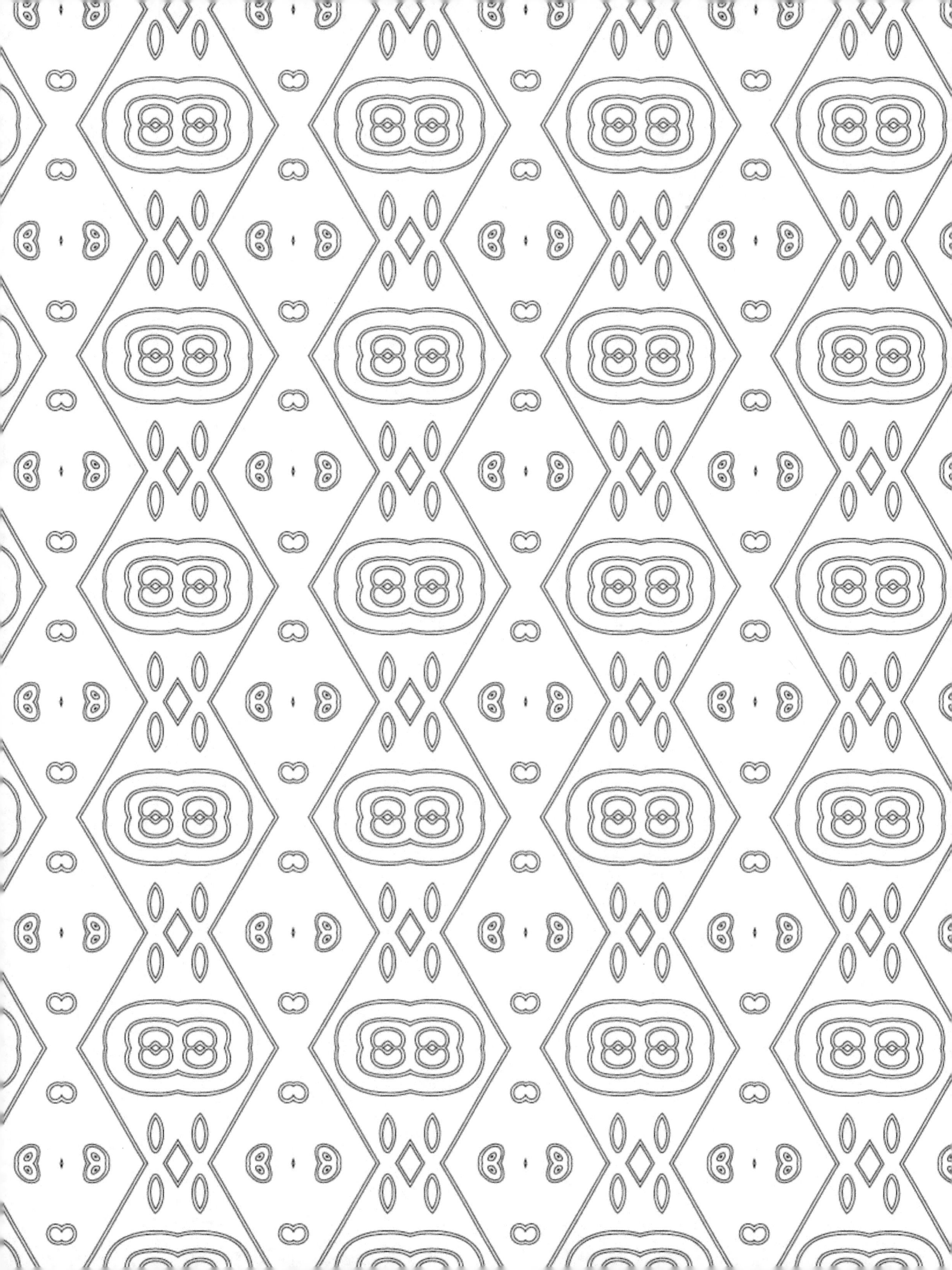

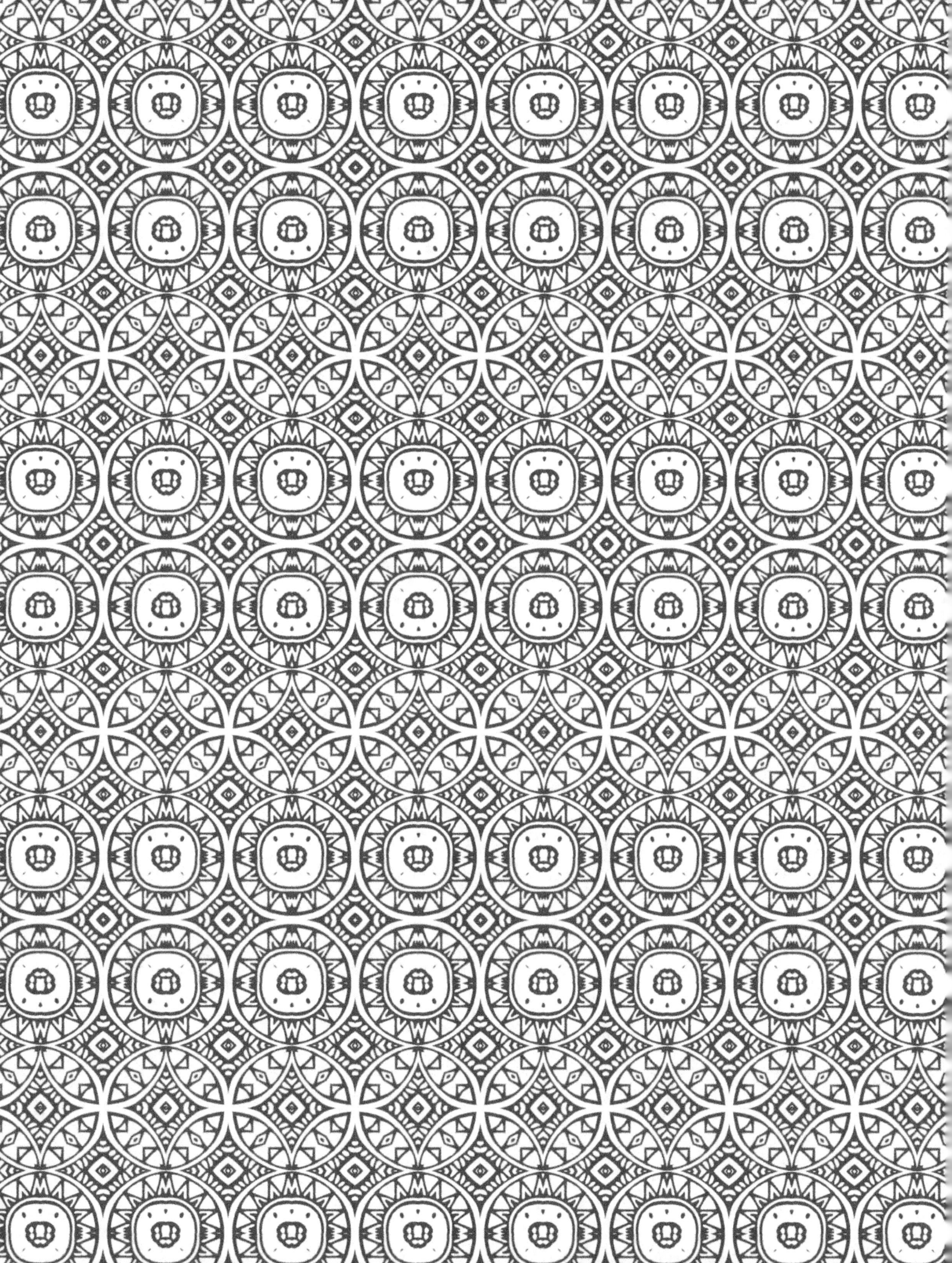

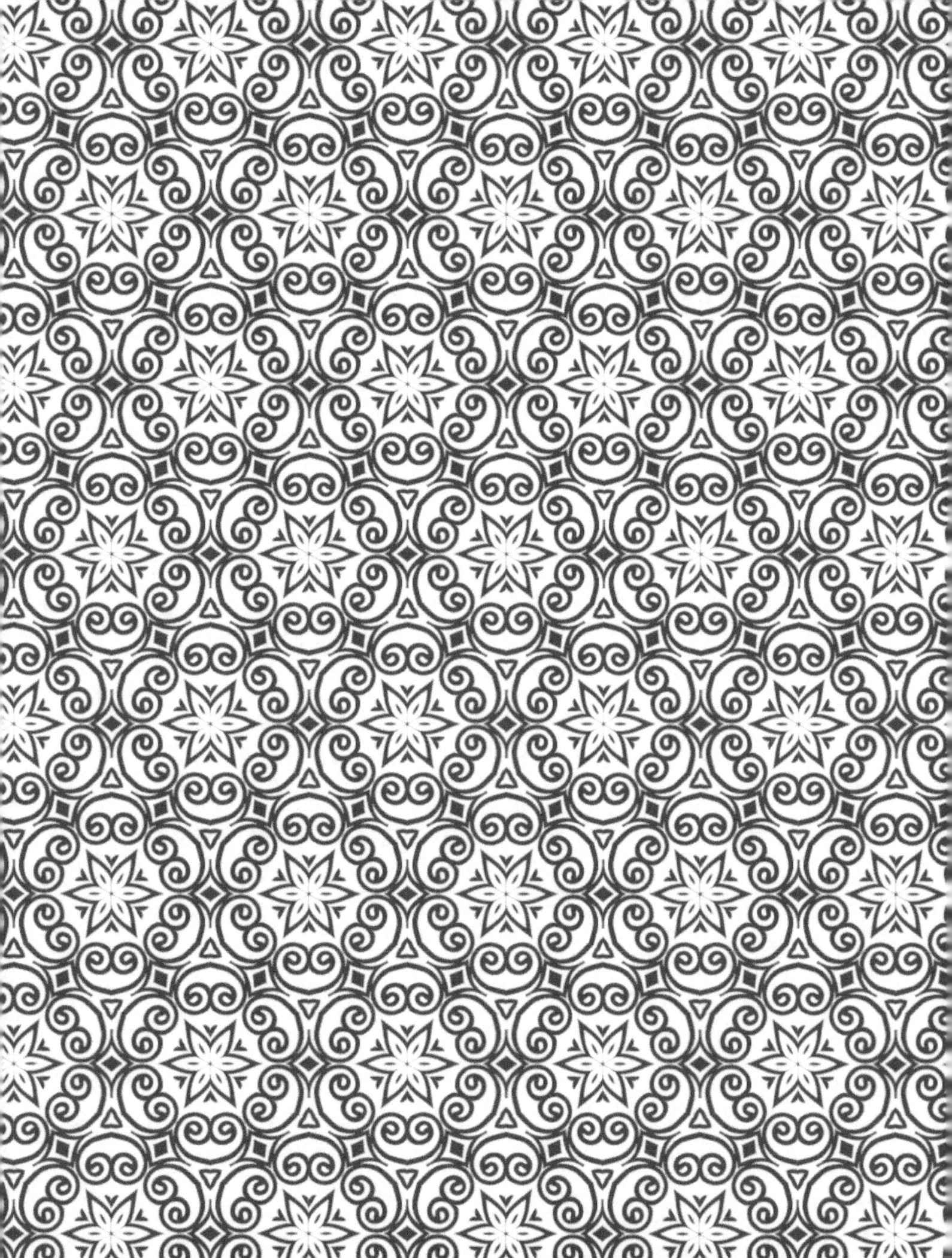

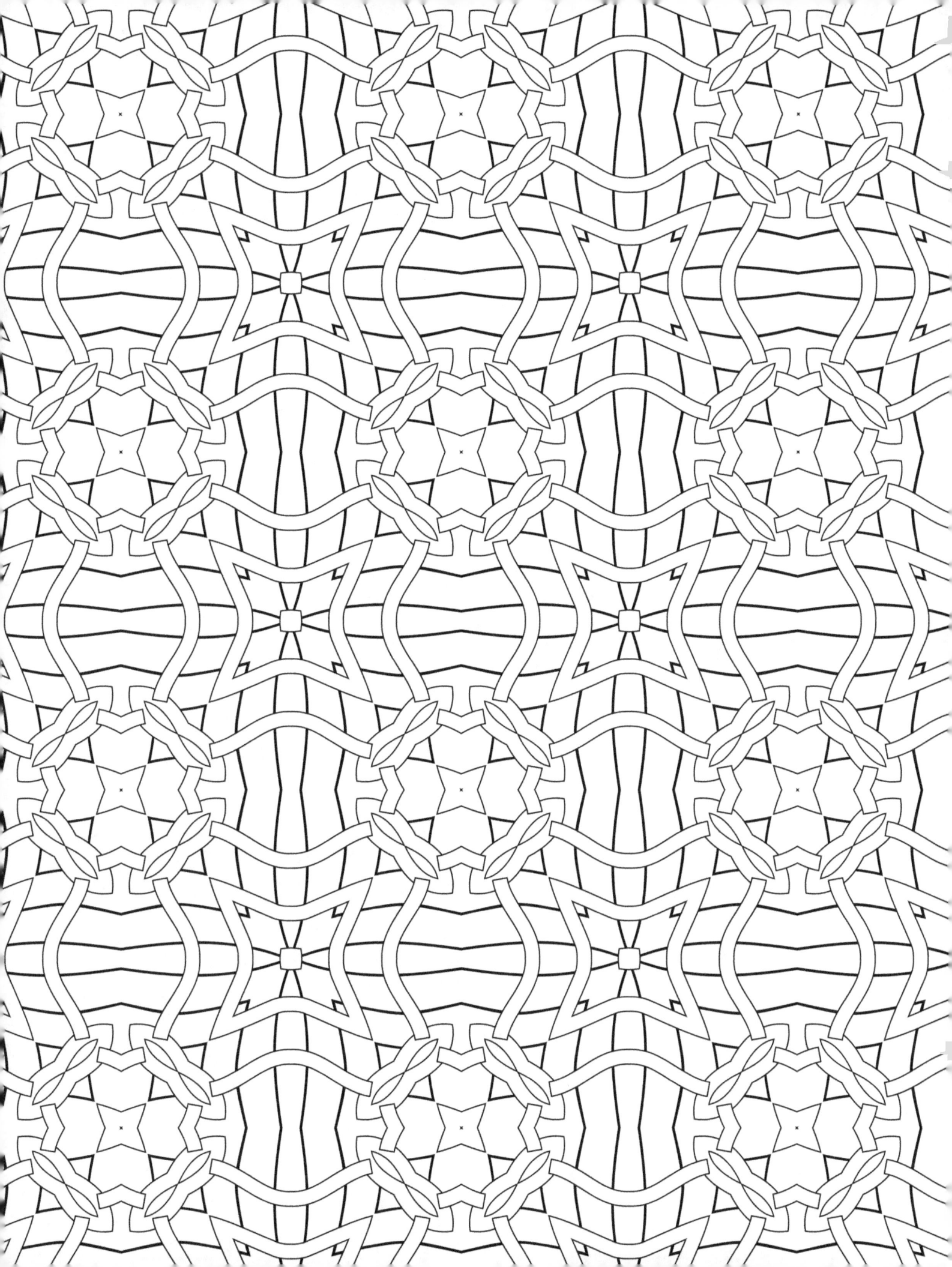

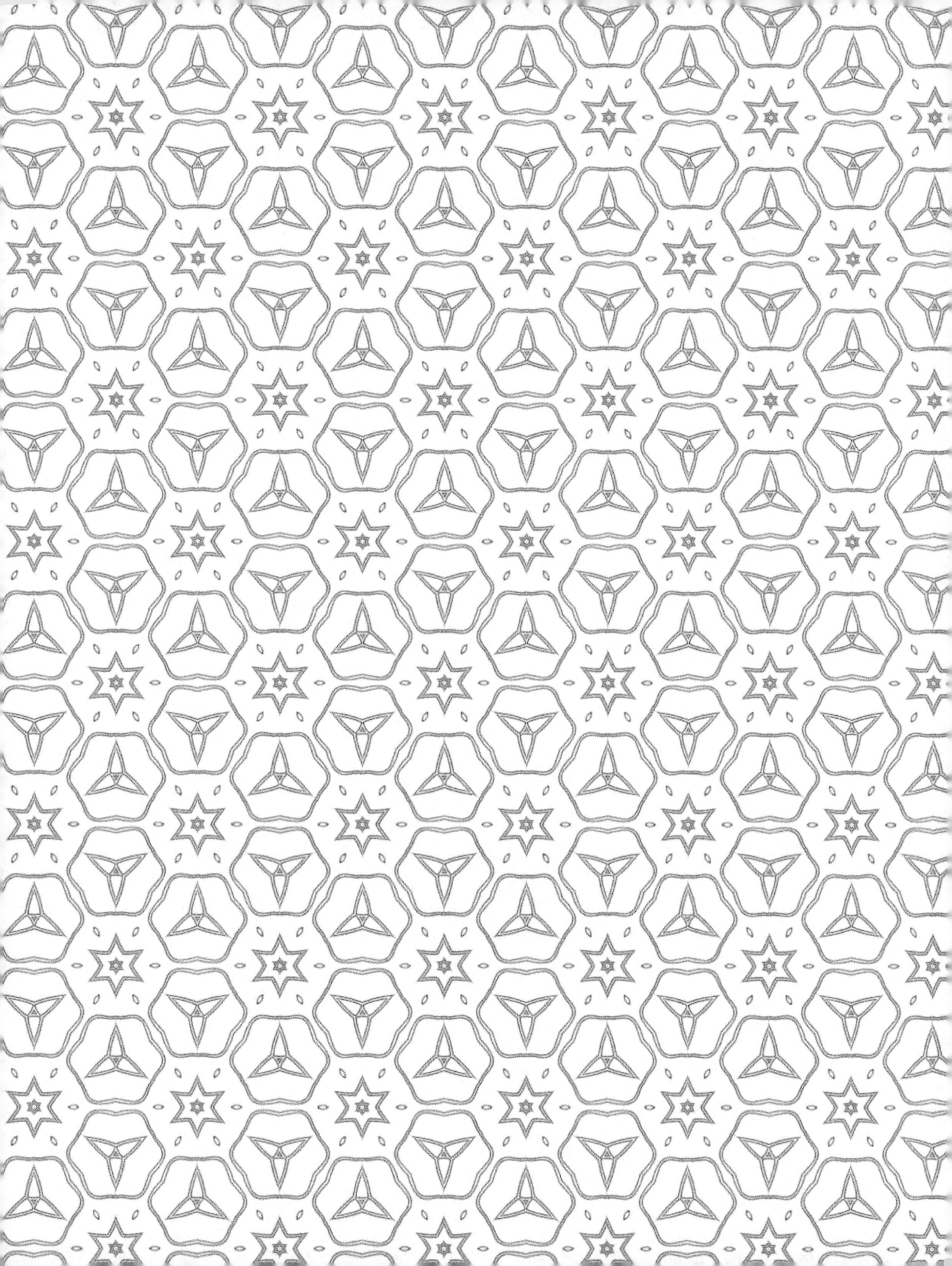

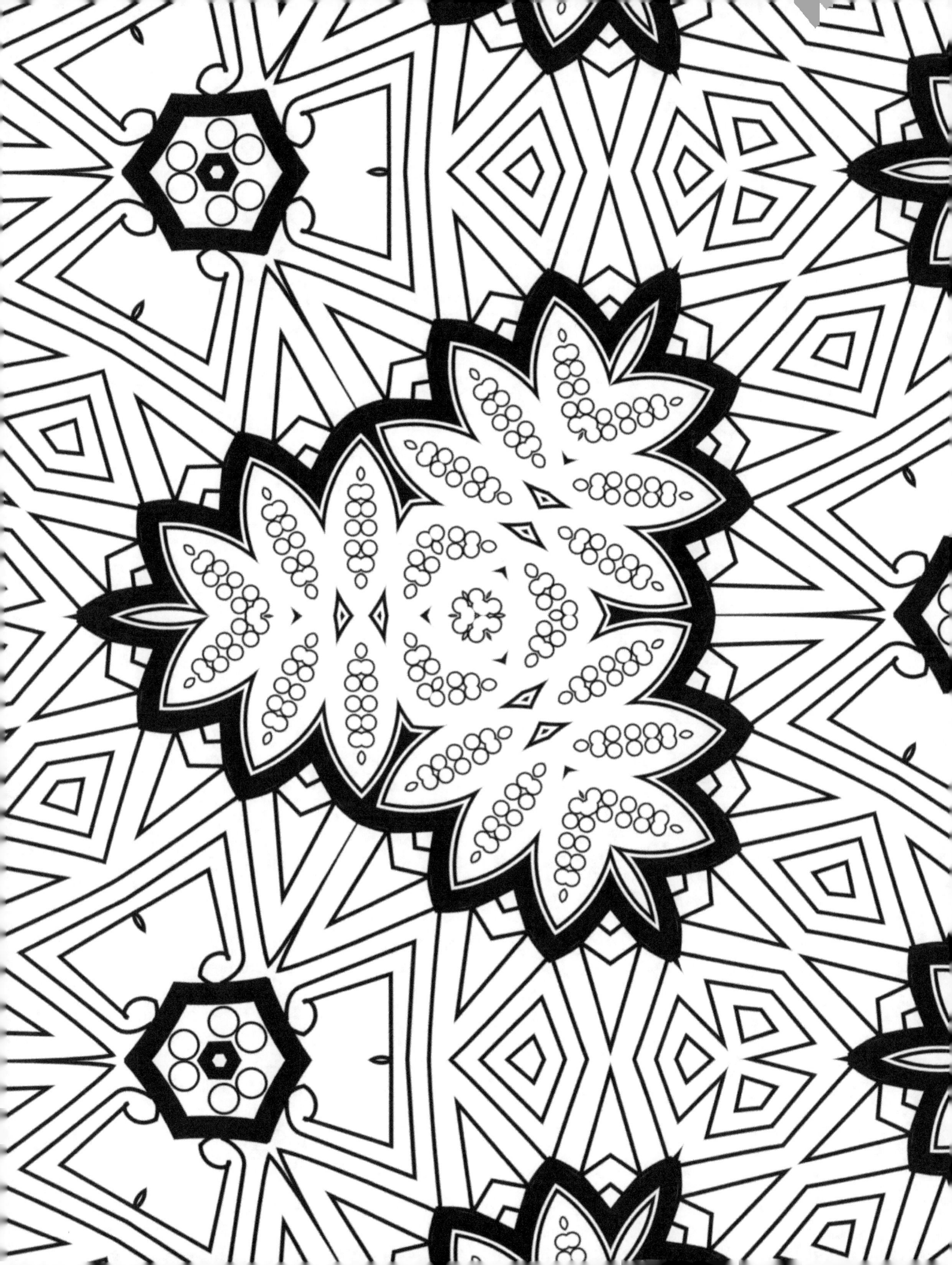

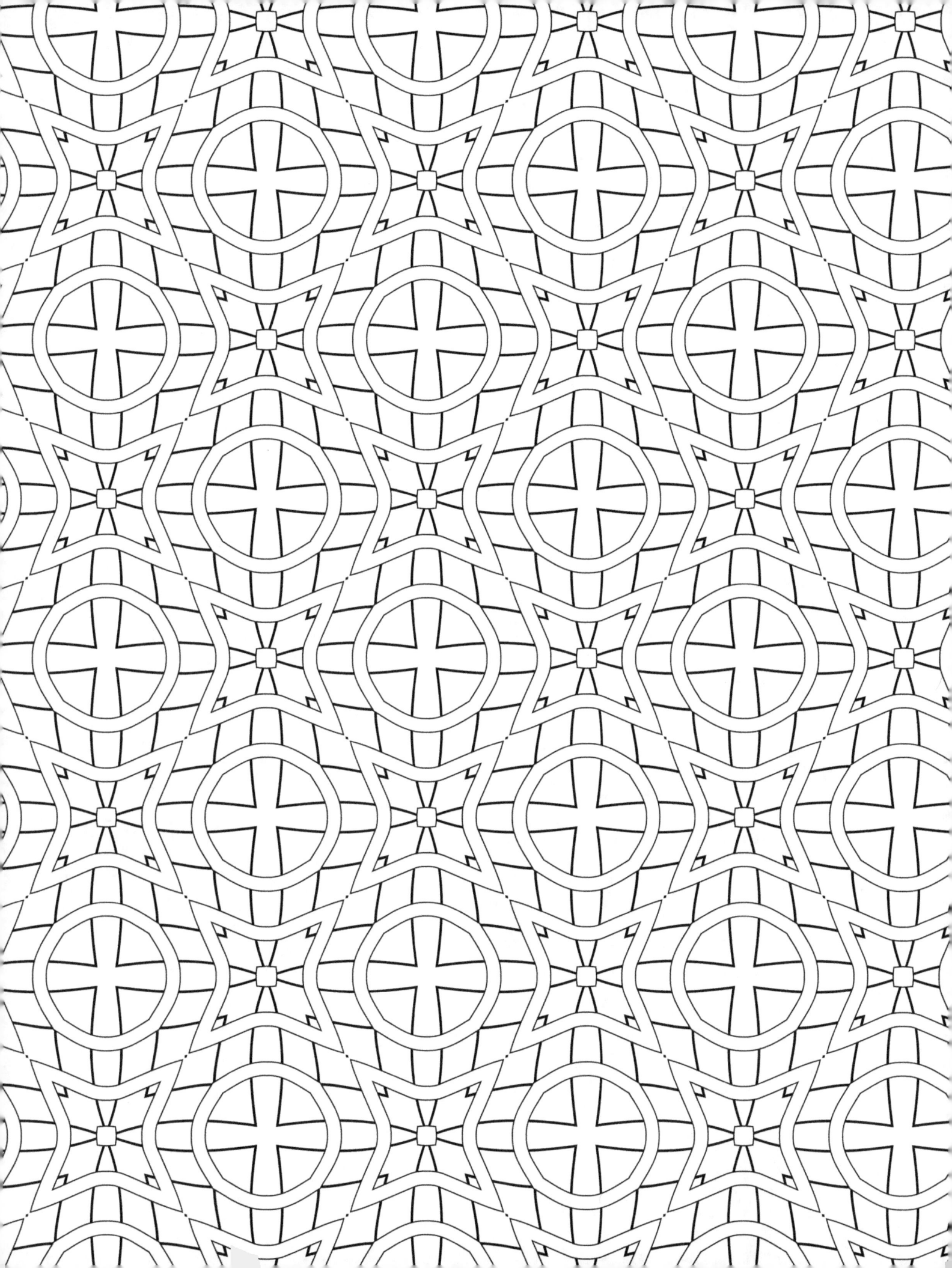

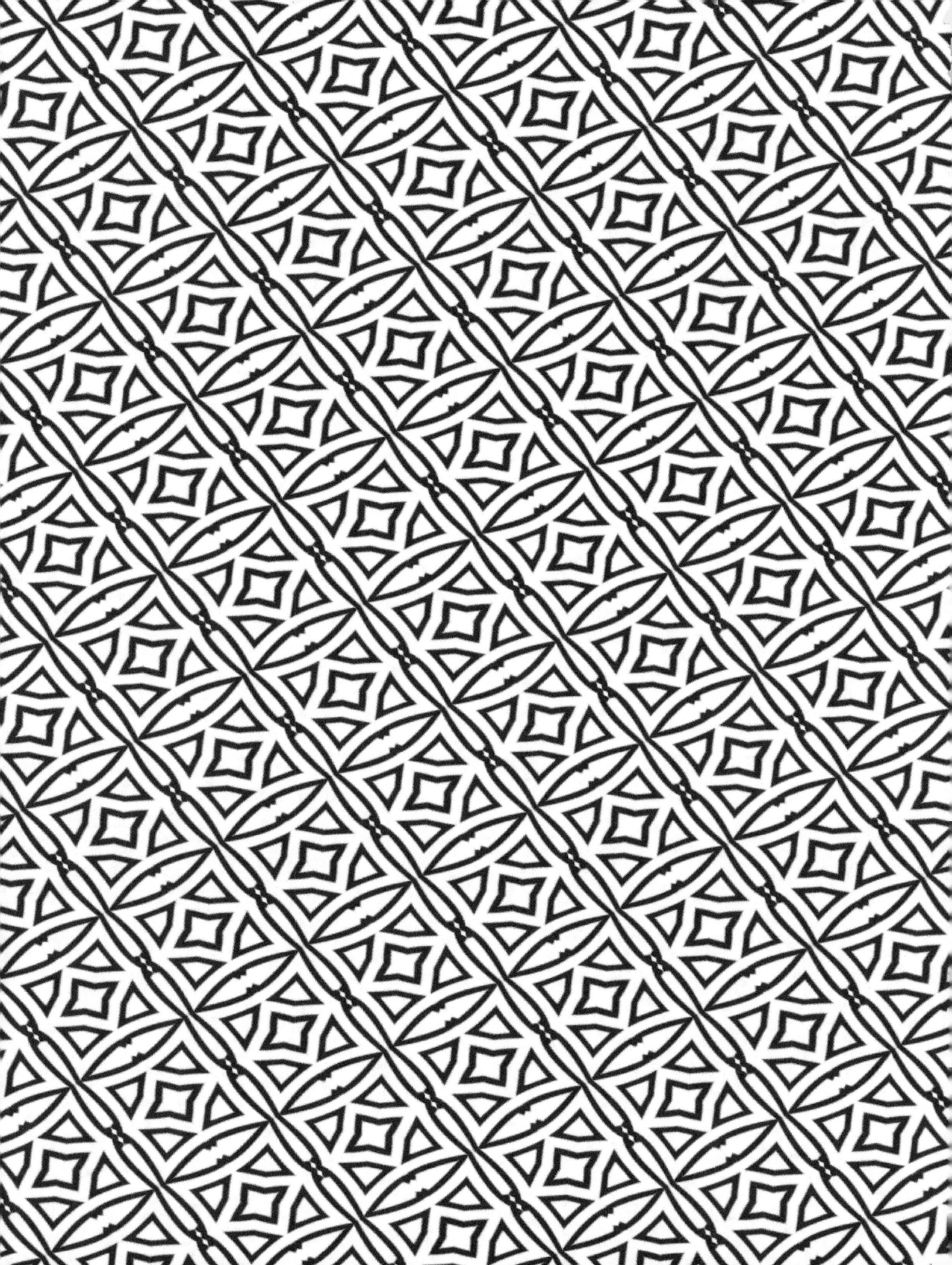

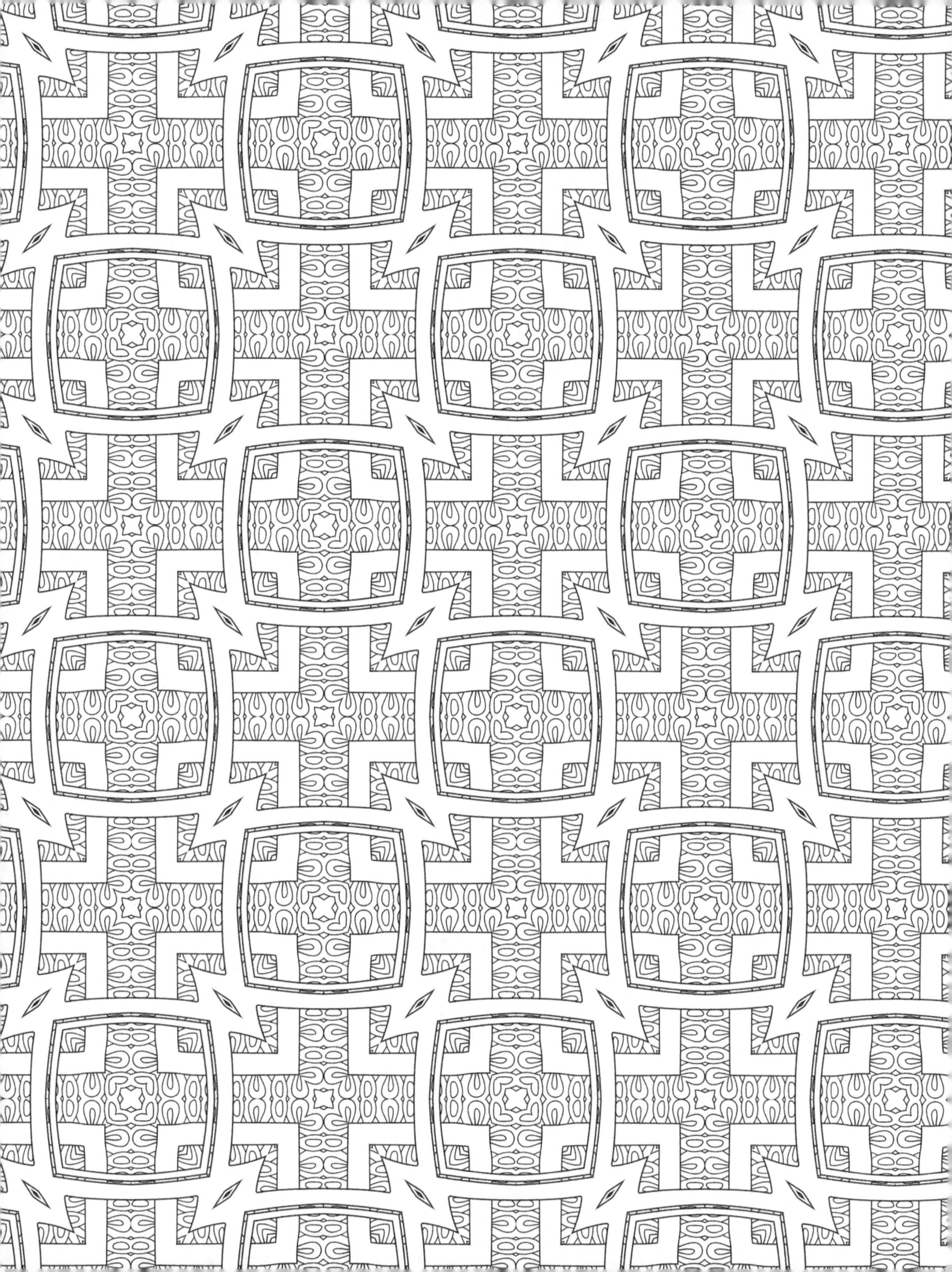

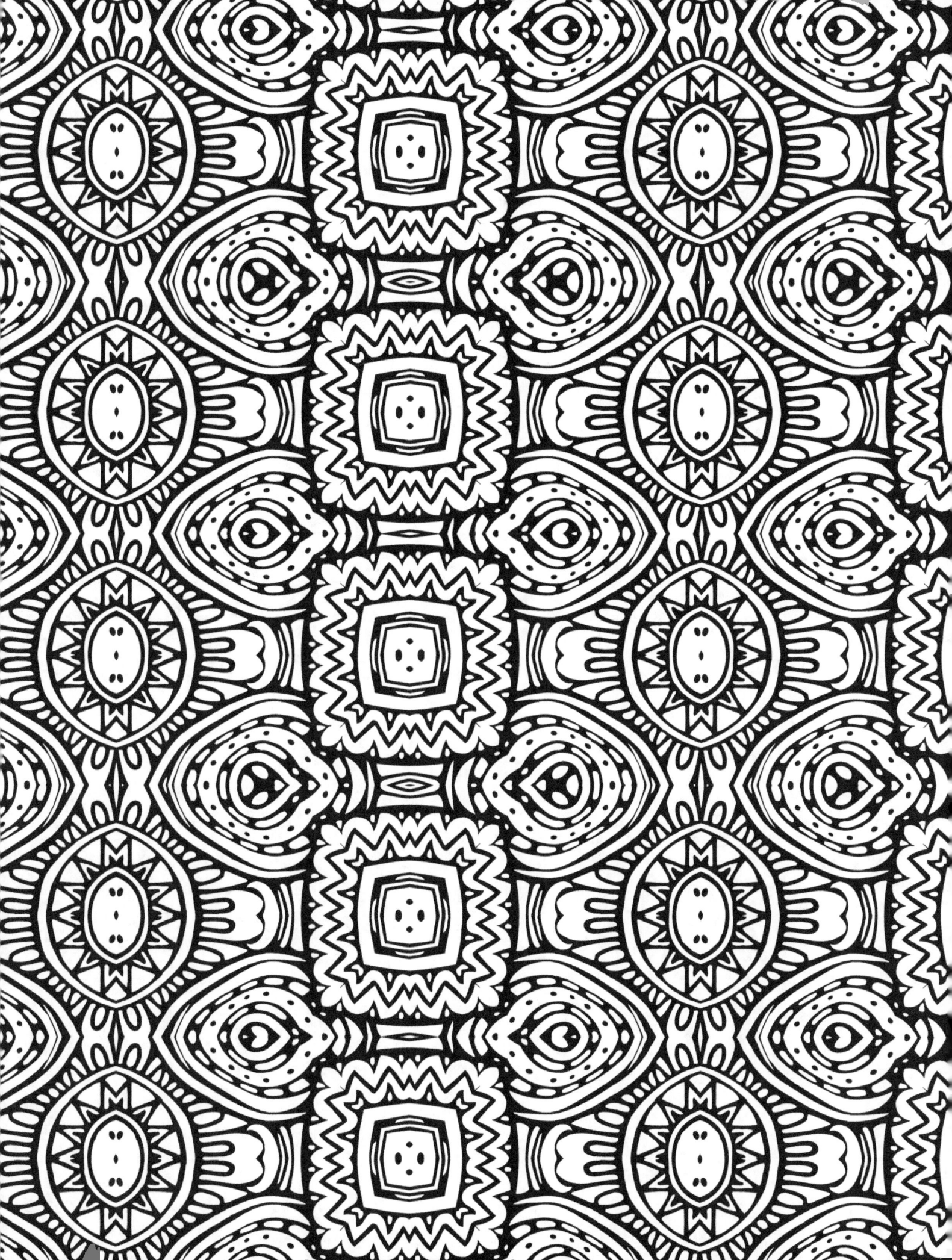

www.ingramcontent.com/pod-product-compliance
Lightning Source LLC
Chambersburg PA
CBHW080540190526
45169CB00007B/2576